MW00974318

How To Be a PRAYiNG

Girl of God

AN INTERACTIVE JOURNAL
INSPIRED BY EXTRAORDINARY
WOMEN OF FAITH

SHILOH kidz
An Imprint of Barbour Publishing, Inc.

Interior illustrations by: Sumiti Collina, Thais Damiao, Aaliya Jaleel, Wendy Leach, Maria Maldonado, Mona Meslier, Isabel Muñoz, Sonya Abby Soekarno

Published by Shiloh Kidz, an imprint of Barbour Publishing, Inc., 1810 Barbour Drive, Uhrichsville, Ohio 44683, www.shilohkidz.com

Our mission is to inspire the world with the life-changing message of the Bible.

 Member of the
Evangelical Christian
Publishers Association

Printed in China.

000157 0320 HA

CONTENTS

You can be a praying Girl of God!

Yes...*YOU!*

Featuring brief stories of dozens of women—from the Bible, throughout history, and today—you'll be inspired to become a praying girl too, as you learn from the examples of strong women of faith—including Esther, Lottie Moon, Ruth, Mary Slessor, Corrie ten Boom, the woman at the well, and dozens more!

Each section will prompt you to

1. Read the short story (read the complete story of each Bible woman in your very own Bible!)

2. Draw a related picture

3. Journal your thoughts about praying women

4. Think about how you can be a praying girl too!

Let's get started! Turn the page to begin your very own courageous journey of prayer!

ANNA

READ THE STORY OF ANNA IN YOUR BIBLE. YOU'LL FIND IT IN LUKE 2:36–38.

Young Anna's husband died early in their marriage, leaving her all alone. Anna turned to God for comfort, spending many hours every day talking with Him. She grew so close to God that she learned to recognize His voice in her heart. One day when Anna was very old, God sent her to the temple to meet a special baby—His Son, Jesus. When Anna saw the baby, she already knew who He was. She prayed and gave thanks to God. Then Anna spent the rest of her life telling others the Good News!

Draw a picture from Anna's story.

Anna's story is important because. . .

I can be a praying girl of God, like Anna, when. . .

_____

_____

_____

_____

_____

_____

_____

_____

_____

_____

_____

_____

_____

_____

_____

_____

_____

_____

_____

_____

_____

_____

_____

> *"Then you will call upon Me and come and pray to Me, and I will listen to you."*
>
> JEREMIAH 29:12

MARY MCLEOD BETHUNE

(1875–1955)

When Mary McLeod Bethune was just a girl, she watched her parents struggle to make a life free from slavery. She wanted to learn to read and write, and so she asked God to make a way for her dreams to come true. And God answered Mary's prayer! She graduated from college and became a teacher. Mary wanted to provide the very best education for all African American children, so she opened a school. And for the rest of her life, Mary made it her mission to help African Americans gain equality.

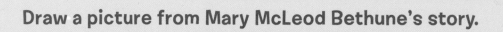

Draw a picture from Mary McLeod Bethune's story.

Mary McLeod Bethune's story is important because. . .

_____

_____

_____

_____

_____

_____

_____

_____

_____

_____

_____

_____

_____

_____

_____

_____

_____

_____

_____

_____

_____

I can be a praying girl of God, like Mary McLeod Bethune, when. . .

_____

_____

_____

_____

_____

_____

_____

_____

_____

_____

_____

_____

_____

_____

_____

_____

_____

_____

_____

> *"For I know the plans I have for you,"* says the Lord, *"plans for well-being and not for trouble, to give you a future and a hope."*
>
> JEREMIAH 29:11

THE CANAANITE WOMAN

READ THE STORY OF THE CANAANITE WOMAN IN YOUR BIBLE.
YOU'LL FIND IT IN MATTHEW 15:21–28.

The Canaanite woman's daughter was very sick. She believed that Jesus could heal her daughter, so she asked for His help. Jesus ignored her when she first called out to Him, but she didn't give up. She went to Him and got on her knees and prayed, "Lord, help me!" She believed Jesus would give her what she wanted. Jesus was testing the Canaanite woman's faith—and He saw it was very strong indeed, and so He healed her daughter right away.

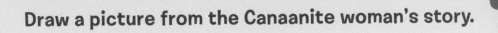

Draw a picture from the Canaanite woman's story.

The Canaanite woman's story is important because. . .

_____
_____
_____
_____
_____
_____
_____
_____
_____
_____
_____
_____
_____
_____
_____
_____
_____
_____
_____
_____
_____

I can be a praying girl of God,
like the Canaanite woman, when. . .

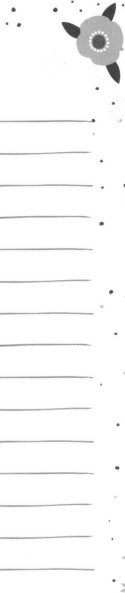

_____

_____

_____

_____

_____

_____

_____

_____

_____

_____

_____

_____

_____

_____

_____

_____

_____

_____

_____

_____

_____

> *Learn well how to wait so you will be strong and complete and in need of nothing.*
>
> JAMES 1:4

AMY CARMICHAEL

(1867–1951)

When Amy Carmichael was a little girl, she asked God to make her brown eyes blue. Imagine her disappointment when her eyes stayed brown! As Amy grew in her faith, so did her desire to become a missionary. She prayed, and God told her to go—first to Japan and later to India. Young girls in India were often kidnapped, so Amy helped hide them. She disguised herself to look like an Indian woman. Most had brown eyes, just like hers, which helped her to blend in among the people instead of standing out. Amy remembered her childhood prayer and understood why God had given her brown eyes!

Draw a picture from Amy Carmichael's story.

Amy Carmichael's story is important because. . .

_____
_____
_____
_____
_____
_____
_____
_____
_____
_____
_____
_____
_____
_____
_____
_____
_____
_____
_____
_____
_____

I can be a praying girl of God, like Amy Carmichael, when. . .

> *Trust in the Lord with all your heart, and do not trust in your own understanding. Agree with Him in all your ways, and He will make your paths straight.*
>
> PROVERBS 3:5–6

FANNY CROSBY

(1820–1915)

Fanny Crosby, who had been blind almost since birth, didn't allow blindness to stop her from writing or doing anything else she set her mind to. Her poetry gave her the opportunity to meet presidents, governors, and other famous people. Fanny's poems were even published in books, but none made Fanny famous until she began writing lyrics for hymns and Sunday school songs. Soon almost everyone knew her name. Sometimes Fanny needed ideas for her lyrics. And when she asked God for help, the ideas came! Fanny Crosby wrote nearly nine thousand hymns in her lifetime!

Draw a picture from Fanny Crosby's story.

Fanny Crosby's story is important because. . .

_____

_____

_____

_____

_____

_____

_____

_____

_____

_____

_____

_____

_____

_____

_____

_____

_____

_____

_____

_____

_____

_____

_____

I can be a praying girl of God, like Fanny Crosby, when...

Everything comes from [God].

ROMANS 11:36

DEBORAH

READ THE STORY OF DEBORAH IN YOUR BIBLE.
YOU'LL FIND IT IN JUDGES 4–5.

Deborah was a very wise judge. God spoke to her, and then she told others what He said. She told a warrior named Barak that God wanted him and his troops to fight against an army led by a general named Sisera. Sisera's army was going after the Israelites, and God wanted the Israelites—His people—to be saved. Barak insisted that Deborah go with him, and so she did. And the Israelites won the battle! Deborah thanked God for the victory by singing a song of praise.

Draw a picture from Deborah's story.

Deborah's story is important because. . .

_____

_____

_____

_____

_____

_____

_____

_____

_____

_____

_____

_____

_____

_____

_____

_____

_____

_____

_____

_____

_____

_____

I can be a praying girl of God, like Deborah, when. . .

_____

_____

_____

_____

_____

_____

_____

_____

_____

_____

_____

_____

_____

_____

_____

_____

_____

_____

_____

> *"O give thanks to the Lord. Call upon His name. Let the people know what He has done. Sing to Him. Sing praises to Him. Tell of all His great works."*
>
> 1 CHRONICLES 16:8–9

FAYE EDGERTON

(1889–1968)

Faye Edgerton, an American missionary, wanted to share God's Word with others. While serving a Navajo reservation in Arizona and using an interpreter—someone who knew both English and Navajo—the translation often got messed up because the Bible didn't exist in their language. So Faye, along with her family, prayed that God would help her learn one of the most difficult languages in the world. God heard, and He helped Faye learn. She eventually became a Bible translator. Today the New Testament exists not only in Navajo, but also in more than 1,500 other languages!

Draw a picture from Faye Edgerton's story.

Faye Edgerton's story is important because. . .

_____
_____
_____
_____
_____
_____
_____
_____
_____
_____
_____
_____
_____
_____
_____
_____
_____
_____
_____
_____
_____

I can be a praying girl of God, like Faye Edgerton, when. . .

_____

_____

_____

_____

_____

_____

_____

_____

_____

_____

_____

_____

_____

_____

_____

_____

_____

_____

_____

> *There are many languages in the world. All of them have meaning to the people who understand them.*
>
> 1 CORINTHIANS 14:10

ESTHER

READ THE STORY OF ESTHER IN YOUR BIBLE.
YOU'LL FIND IT IN ESTHER 2:1–9:32.

Esther, a Jewish orphan, lived with her cousin Mordecai in a time when their king was searching for a wife. The king chose Esther to be his queen! One of the king's men, Haman, hated Jews. He made up lies and convinced the king to have all the Jews killed. Esther worried that if she talked to the king about it, she might die with the rest of her people. Esther told Mordecai to have all the Jews pray for her, and she would pray too. Esther trusted in the power of prayer. When she revealed to the king that she was Jewish and asked him to save her people, he agreed. And in the end, he punished Haman for his lies!

Draw a picture from Esther's story.

Esther's story is important because. . .

I can be a praying girl of God, like Esther, when. . .

_____

_____

_____

_____

_____

_____

_____

_____

_____

_____

_____

_____

_____

_____

_____

_____

_____

_____

_____

_____

_____

Do not worry. Learn to pray about everything.
Give thanks to God as you ask
Him for what you need.

PHILIPPIANS 4:6

MORROW GRAHAM

(1892–1981)

Do you know who Billy Graham is? He was a famous preacher who led many people to the Lord. Billy's mother, Morrow Graham, made sure her kids knew about Jesus. She prayed for her children all the time, and she wrote many letters to her son when he was in Bible school. In fact, on the day Billy went away to school, she asked God to help her write letters that would encourage and help him. One of Billy's letters to his mom said he especially appreciated the cheerful letters she wrote to him. God answered Mrs. Graham's prayer!

Draw a picture from Morrow Graham's story.

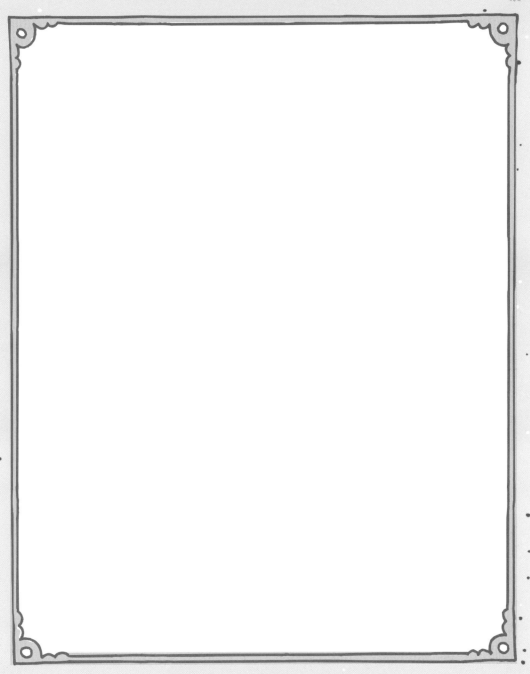

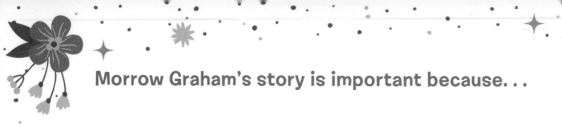

Morrow Graham's story is important because. . .

_____

_____

_____

_____

_____

_____

_____

_____

_____

_____

_____

_____

_____

_____

_____

_____

_____

_____

_____

_____

_____

I can be a praying girl of God, like Morrow Graham, when. . .

_____

_____

_____

_____

_____

_____

_____

_____

_____

_____

_____

_____

_____

_____

_____

_____

_____

_____

_____

_____

_____

> *"For where two or three are gathered together in My name, there I am with them."*
>
> MATTHEW 18:20

HANNAH

READ THE STORY OF HANNAH IN YOUR BIBLE.
YOU'LL FIND IT IN 1 SAMUEL 1; 2:1–21.

Hannah wanted a baby. She was often picked on because she had no children. The bullying made Hannah sad. But instead of feeling sorry for herself, Hannah went to the temple and prayed to God. She told God if He gave her a son, she would share the boy with Him. Hannah promised to allow the temple priests to raise her son so he would grow up learning to serve his heavenly Father. God answered Hannah's prayer and gave her what she wanted. And Hannah kept her promise to God. Her son, Samuel, grew up to be a great man. He became a priest, a judge, and a prophet and is remembered even today for his wisdom.

Draw a picture from Hannah's story.

Hannah's story is important because. . .

_____

_____

_____

_____

_____

_____

_____

_____

_____

_____

_____

_____

_____

_____

_____

_____

_____

_____

_____

_____

_____

_____

_____

I can be a praying girl of God, like Hannah, when. . .

_____

_____

_____

_____

_____

_____

_____

_____

_____

_____

_____

_____

_____

_____

_____

_____

_____

> *"You must give your whole heart to him and hold out your hands to him for help."*
>
> JOB 11:13 NCV

ANNE HUTCHINSON

(1591–1643)

Anne Hutchinson's parents raised her to think for herself and question others' beliefs—even if it wasn't the popular thing to do. When she grew up and got married, Anne and her husband moved across the ocean from England to the Massachusetts Bay Colony in America. There, the governor wanted everyone to follow strict Puritan rules—which included that women were to keep their beliefs quiet while men took the lead. Anne disagreed and decided she wasn't going to keep quiet! She led prayer meetings in her house and shared her faith with others. She was one of the first American women to speak up about her faith.

Draw a picture from Anne Hutchinson's story.

Anne Hutchinson's story is important because. . .

I can be a praying girl of God, like Anne Hutchinson, when. . .

_____

_____

_____

_____

_____

_____

_____

_____

_____

_____

_____

_____

_____

_____

_____

_____

_____

_____

_____

_____

_____

> *"Be strong and have strength of heart.*
> *Do not be afraid or shake with fear...*
> *For the Lord your God is the*
> *One Who goes with you."*
>
> DEUTERONOMY 31:6

JOCHEBED

READ THE STORY OF JOCHEBED IN YOUR BIBLE.
YOU'LL FIND IT IN EXODUS 1; 2:1–10.

Egypt's king hated Jews, and so he ordered his people to drown all the Jewish baby boys. Jochebed had a newborn son, and she was determined to keep him alive. As her baby grew bigger, hiding him became difficult. Jochebed decided to trust God with her son's life. She put her baby in a basket and set it in tall grass by the Nile River. Then she told her daughter, Miriam, to hide and watch. We can imagine that in that moment, Jochebed prayed mighty prayers. And God worked it out for good! The king's daughter found the baby and decided to save him. The baby grew up to be Moses, one of the Jews' greatest heroes.

Draw a picture from Jochebed's story.

Jochebed's story is important because. . .

_____
_____
_____
_____
_____
_____
_____
_____
_____
_____
_____
_____
_____
_____
_____
_____
_____
_____
_____
_____
_____

I can be a praying girl of God, like Jochebed, when. . .

_____

_____

_____

_____

_____

_____

_____

_____

_____

_____

_____

_____

_____

_____

_____

_____

_____

_____

_____

_____

We know that God makes all things work together for the good of those who love Him and are chosen to be a part of His plan.

ROMANS 8:28

TAMARA JOLEE (METCALFE)

(1980–)

Tamara Jolee is an award-winning reporter. Out of all the stories she tells, the one she shares most often is about how God is helping her live with a serious illness—a blood cancer that could take her life. Everything was going very well in her career when Tamara received the devastating news about her health, and it would have made sense if she had asked God, "Why me?" But instead, she prayed, "Lord, what's next?" And when she asked God that question, Tamara felt peace. God was telling her that whatever happened, it would be okay. Tamara trusts Jesus to lead her, and she is at peace knowing that He is on her side.

Draw a picture from Tamara Jolee's story.

Tamara Jolee's story is important because. . .

_____

_____

_____

_____

_____

_____

_____

_____

_____

_____

_____

_____

_____

_____

_____

_____

_____

_____

_____

_____

_____

_____

I can be a praying girl of God, like Tamara Jolee, when. . .

> *The peace of God is much greater than the human mind can understand. This peace will keep your hearts and minds through Christ Jesus.*
>
> PHILIPPIANS 4:7

ANN HASSELTINE JUDSON

(1789-1826)

When Ann Hasseltine committed her life to God and asked Him where He wanted her to go, God heard. She would become the first woman missionary overseas! Ann and her husband, Adoniram Judson, went to Burma—the people there hadn't heard about Jesus. They had a very difficult time explaining the Good News of Jesus in the Burmese language. But Ann was determined to figure it out. She translated the Gospel so the people could understand, and one by one, they began surrendering their lives to Jesus. Ann wrote about her missionary work, and her stories influenced many women to become missionaries in faraway lands too.

Draw a picture from Ann Hasseltine Judson's story.

Ann Hasseltine Judson's story is important because. . .

_____

_____

_____

_____

_____

_____

_____

_____

_____

_____

_____

_____

_____

_____

_____

_____

_____

_____

_____

_____

_____

_____

_____

I can be a praying girl of God, like Ann Hasseltine Judson, when. . .

_____

_____

_____

_____

_____

_____

_____

_____

_____

_____

_____

_____

_____

_____

_____

_____

_____

_____

_____

Then Jesus said to them all, "If anyone wants to follow Me, he must give up himself and his own desires. He must take up his cross everyday and follow Me."

LUKE 9:23

MARY LYON

(1797–1849)

Nineteen-year-old Mary Lyon walked up a hill near her house so she could spend time alone with God. She prayed, giving her life to God and asking Him to guide her forever. She felt God leading her to raise money to start her own school, a college for girls. She named it Mount Holyoke. There, girls learned science, math, and other subjects. But Mary required them to attend church and Bible study too. She also set aside quiet time so her girls could be alone and pray. Mount Holyoke still exists as a women's college today. Many graduates of the school became leaders who went on to inspire others—all thanks to God, Mary, and her hilltop prayer.

Draw a picture from Mary Lyon's story.

Mary Lyon's story is important because. . .

I can be a praying girl of God, like Mary Lyon, when. . .

We are sure that if we ask anything that He wants us to have, He will hear us.

1 JOHN 5:14

MARTHA

READ THE STORY OF MARTHA IN YOUR BIBLE.
YOU'LL FIND IT IN JOHN 11:1–45.

Jesus had three very close friends, Lazarus and his sisters, Mary and Martha. They all trusted Jesus, believing He would be there to help whenever they needed Him. One day, Lazarus got very sick and died before Jesus came. (His sisters had sent for Jesus, but He didn't come right away.) Martha said, "Lord, if You had been here, my brother would not have died. I know even now God will give You whatever You ask" (vv. 21–22). Jesus did a miracle that day and raised Lazarus from the dead. The stone was rolled away from the tomb, and Lazarus walked out—alive and well!

Draw a picture from Martha's story.

Martha's story is important because. . .

_____
_____
_____
_____
_____
_____
_____
_____
_____
_____
_____
_____
_____
_____
_____
_____
_____
_____
_____
_____
_____
_____

I can be a praying girl of God, like Martha, when. . .

> *The Lord is good to those who wait for Him, to the one who looks for Him. It is good that one should be quiet and wait for the saving power of the Lord.*
>
> LAMENTATIONS 3:25–26

MARY, MOTHER OF JESUS

READ THE STORY OF MARY, MOTHER OF JESUS, IN YOUR BIBLE.
YOU'LL FIND IT IN LUKE 1:28–35, 46–55.

An angel came to deliver an exciting message to Mary: she was chosen by God to give birth to baby Jesus. Mary didn't know why God had chosen her. The angel only said, "You are honored very much. You are a favored woman. The Lord is with you. You are chosen from among many women" (v. 28). Imagine what went through Mary's mind! Instead of panicking and giving reasons why she shouldn't be the one to do it, she thanked God. She said, "My heart sings with thanks for my Lord. And my spirit is happy in God, the One Who saves from the punishment of sin.... He Who is powerful has done great things for me" (vv. 46–47, 49).

Draw a picture from the story of Mary, mother of Jesus.

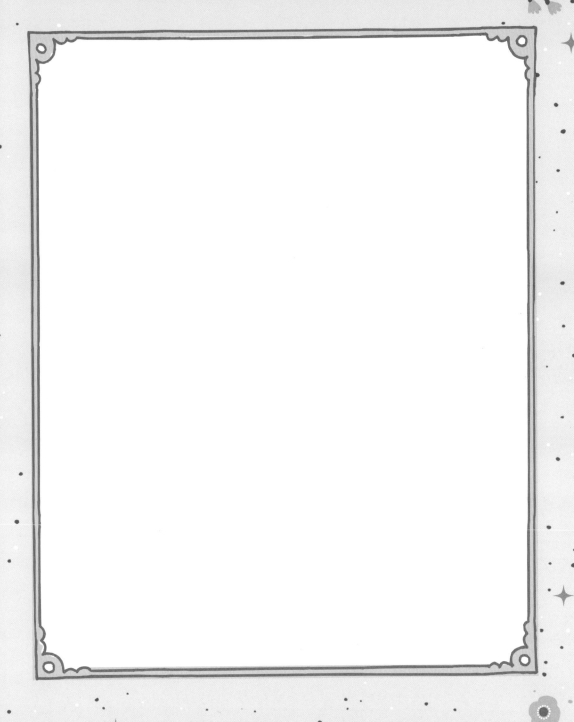

The story of Mary, mother of Jesus, is important because...

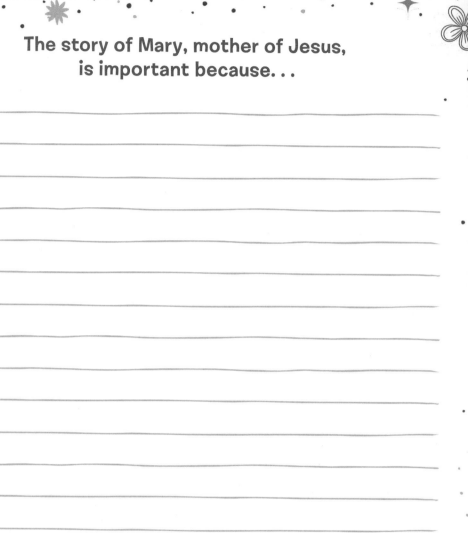

I can be a praying girl of God, like Mary, mother of Jesus, when. . .

_____

_____

_____

_____

_____

_____

_____

_____

_____

_____

_____

_____

_____

_____

_____

_____

_____

_____

_____

_____

_____

> *Be full of joy all the time. Never stop praying. In everything give thanks. This is what God wants you to do because of Christ Jesus.*
>
> 1 THESSALONIANS 5:16–18

MARY OF BETHANY

READ THE STORY OF MARY OF BETHANY IN YOUR BIBLE.
YOU'LL FIND IT IN LUKE 10:38–42.

Jesus was on His way to visit Mary and Martha. The sisters looked forward to His visits, and when they heard He was coming, they got busy. But when Jesus arrived, Mary stopped working. While Martha cooked, Mary sat with Jesus. She listened carefully to everything He said. This made Martha unhappy. She said to Jesus, "Do You see that my sister is not helping me? Tell her to help me." Jesus answered, "Martha, Martha, you are worried and troubled about many things. Only a few things are important, even just one. Mary has chosen the good thing. It will not be taken away from her" (vv. 40–42).

Draw a picture from Mary of Bethany's story.

Mary of Bethany's story is important because...

_____

_____

_____

_____

_____

_____

_____

_____

_____

_____

_____

_____

_____

_____

_____

_____

_____

_____

_____

_____

_____

_____

_____

I can be a praying girl of God, like Mary of Bethany, when. . .

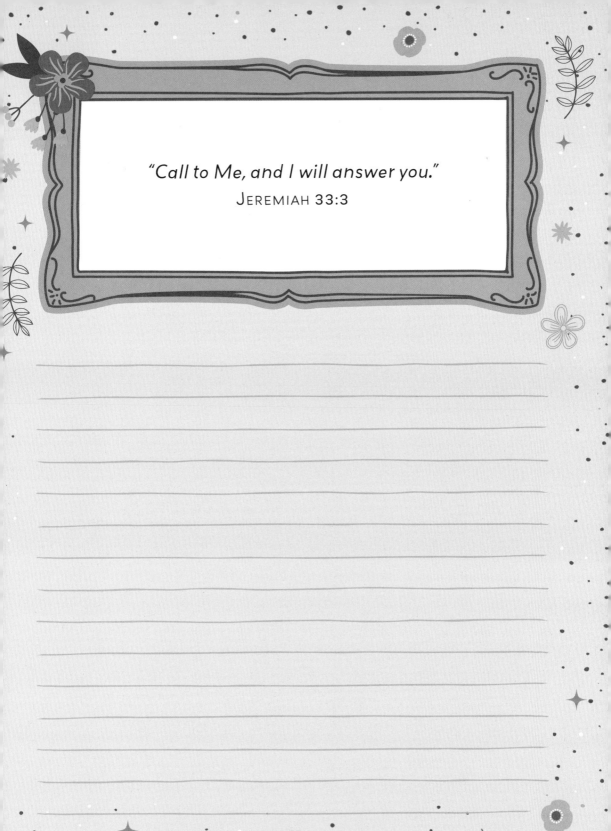

"Call to Me, and I will answer you."

JEREMIAH 33:3

MIRIAM

READ THE STORY OF MIRIAM IN YOUR BIBLE.
YOU'LL FIND IT IN EXODUS 15:20–21.

Miriam was Moses' sister. She was with him when he led the Israelites out of Egypt, where Pharaoh held them as slaves. As Moses led the Israelites away, Pharaoh's army chased them all the way to the Red Sea. When Moses and the Israelites got there, God parted the sea and opened up a dry pathway for them to walk through. When they arrived safely on the other side, God closed the path, and the sea swallowed up Pharaoh's army! Miriam led the women in praise. "Miriam said to them, 'Sing to the Lord, for He is praised for His greatness. He has thrown the horse and horseman into the sea' " (v. 21). The women were so filled with joyfulness that they played tambourines, sang, and danced, praising God for His goodness.

Draw a picture from Miriam's story.

Miriam's story is important because. . .

_____

_____

_____

_____

_____

_____

_____

_____

_____

_____

_____

_____

_____

_____

_____

_____

_____

_____

_____

_____

I can be a praying girl of God, like Miriam, when. . .

I will be glad and full of joy because of You.
I will sing praise to Your name, O Most High.

PSALM 9:2

LOTTIE MOON

(1840–1912)

Lottie Moon grew up in Virginia in the 1840s. Her family was Baptist, but Lottie wasn't sure she believed in Jesus. Lottie did well in school, but she caused a lot of trouble. Her Christian friends put Lottie on their prayer list, asking God to save her from sin. Lottie lay awake one night thinking about her behavior, and she prayed and put her trust in Jesus. Lottie's love for the Lord led her to missionary work in China, where few people believed in Jesus. She prayed, and God revealed to her that she needed to be their friend and to *show*, instead of tell, them how to be Christians. So that's what she did. Lottie Moon stayed in China most of her life and encouraged other missionaries to come there too.

Draw a picture from Lottie Moon's story.

Lottie Moon's story is important because. . .

I can be a praying girl of God, like Lottie Moon, when. . .

> *"But I tell you, love those who hate you. (Respect and give thanks for those who say bad things to you. Do good to those who hate you.) Pray for those who do bad things to you and who make it hard for you."*
>
> MATTHEW 5:44

NAOMI

READ THE STORY OF NAOMI IN YOUR BIBLE. YOU'LL FIND IT IN RUTH 1:1–18.

There was no rain, and the crops in Bethlehem died, so Naomi's family moved to Moab. They lived happily for a while until Naomi's husband died. Still, she had her sons to help her. The boys grew up and married women from Moab. But trouble came. Naomi's sons both died. This left Naomi and her daughters-in-law, Orpah and Ruth, with no strong men to help with the everyday hard work. Naomi decided to return to her homeland of Bethlehem. Orpah and Ruth planned to go with her, but Naomi said, "No. Stay here in Moab, where you grew up." Then Naomi prayed an unselfish prayer, asking God to show the women kindness. She was willing to give up the only companions she had so they could have a good life in their homeland. She asked God to bless them!

Draw a picture from Naomi's story.

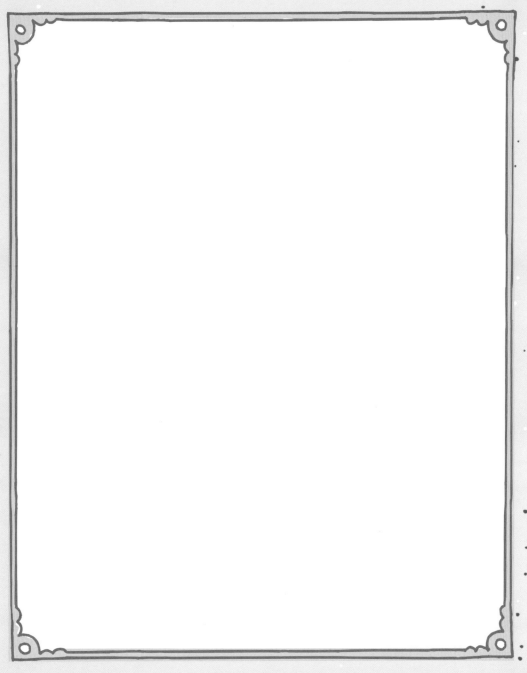

Naomi's story is important because. . .

I can be a praying girl of God, like Naomi, when. . .

> *Pray for the things that are needed.*
> *You must watch and keep on praying.*
> *Remember to pray for all Christians.*
>
> EPHESIANS 6:18

PANDITA RAMABAI

(1858-1922)

Pandita was born into a Hindu family in India. They worshipped gods, goddesses, trees, and animals. While searching for help from these idols, Pandita's father, mother, and sister died of starvation—and Pandita lost faith in her Hindu religion. After Pandita got a scholarship to study medicine in England, she saw Christians in England helping the poor. Because of their example, Pandita discovered how much she needed Jesus herself, and she gave her life to Him. Pandita prayed and traveled the world sharing her faith with others. In India she started Christian "salvation missions." She set up schools, orphanages, and women's shelters to help Indian women learn to live fulfilling, independent lives.

Draw a picture from Pandita Ramabai's story.

Pandita Ramabai's story is important because. . .

_____

_____

_____

_____

_____

_____

_____

_____

_____

_____

_____

_____

_____

_____

_____

_____

_____

_____

_____

_____

_____

I can be a praying girl of God, like Pandita Ramabai, when. . .

_____
_____
_____
_____
_____
_____
_____
_____
_____
_____
_____
_____
_____
_____
_____
_____
_____
_____
_____
_____
_____

> *"Have no gods other than Me."*
>
> EXODUS 20:3

RUTH

READ THE STORY OF RUTH IN YOUR BIBLE.
YOU'LL FIND IT IN RUTH 1–4.

When their husbands died, Naomi told her daughter-in-law Ruth to stay in her homeland, and Ruth did something unselfish in return. She refused to allow Naomi to go home to Bethlehem alone. Ruth promised God that she would never leave Naomi for as long as she lived. And Ruth was blessed with God's kindness. She traveled to Bethlehem with Naomi and met a handsome, rich man named Boaz. They fell in love, got married, and lived happily ever after—and Naomi along with them! God even blessed Ruth with a son, an important part of God's future plan. The little boy grew up to be the grandfather to Israel's greatest king, King David!